Praise for *She Must Be Mad*

'This book of poetry and prose is divine ...
so refreshing yet familiar'
– Cecelia Ahern

'Charly constantly astounds me with how inspired she is ...
[Her] poetry really encapsulates what it is to be a young woman.
All the tensions and anxieties and new discoveries'
– Pandora Sykes

'Prose and poems that have you laughing, crying and questioning your own life in no time'
– *Glamour*

'Thoughtful, funny and wistful'
– *Independent*

'Brave and Beautiful'
– *Stylist*

'Charly's writing is staggeringly impressive'
– *ELLE*

Also by the author

She Must Be Mad

Charly Cox is a 24-year-old writer, producer and poet. Her writing focuses on destigmatizing mental health and the coming-of-age of a young woman surviving the modern world. In January 2017, she published her first poem on Instagram, showing her internet followers her poetry for the first time; since then she's been published on Refinery29, hosted poetry nights and been named by *ELLE* magazine as one of their 20 power players to watch out for in 2018. Charly was named as ambassador for MQ Mental Health in 2018, a charity which funds research into mental illness.

VALIDATE ME

Charly Cox

ONE PLACE. MANY STORIES

HQ
An imprint of HarperCollins*Publishers* Ltd
1 London Bridge Street
London SE1 9GF

This edition 2019

1
First published in Great Britain by
HQ, an imprint of HarperCollins*Publishers* Ltd 2019

ISBN: 978-0-00-834817-5

MIX
Paper from
responsible sources
FSC   FSC™ C007454
www.fsc.org

This book is produced from independently certified FSC™ paper
to ensure responsible forest management.

For more information visit: www.harpercollins.co.uk/green

Typeset by Palimpsest Book Production Limited,
Falkirk, Stirlingshire
Printed and bound in Great Britain by
CPI Group (UK) Ltd, Croydon CR0 4YY

Contents

We are what we pretend to be, so we must be careful about what we pretend to be.

Kurt Vonnegut

Foreword
by Elizabeth Day

I first met Charly Cox in a hotel suite, which makes it sound like an illicit romantic assignation. I suppose, in truth, the reality was not so very far removed given the instantaneous nature of our connection. I loved her straight away, with a ferocity reserved for only the most special of kindred spirits.

I knew her by reputation only, after discovering one of her poems online and finding myself laughing at one line, wincing in recognition by the next and weeping at the last. I followed her on Instagram where she was funny and self-deprecating and talented (and beautiful, of course, but this was the least important). Everything she posted got thousands of likes. Of course it did. Everything she posted was brilliant. Everything she posted had heart.

When I met her IRL, she was even better. Yes, she had heart. But she also had soul. She claimed to be 23 but really I knew she must be lying because her entire being was shot through with the gold thread of wisdom. I had that thing – that curious, embarrassing thing that you barely ever feel when you're grown up – of wanting desperately for this woman to like me back.

We were in the hotel to do a series of readings to mark its opening, while various guests from a party downstairs were shepherded through the suite to listen to us. It was surreal. At one point, Charly was standing in front of a bathtub performing one of her poems while I was perched on the edge of a four-poster bed reading a passage from a novel. Afterwards, we bonded over the glorious weirdness of the evening. Now, she is my dear friend.

So you won't be getting one of those objective, academic forewords where I analyse the cadence and rhythm of her language, wonderful though it is. No, this is a wholeheartedly subjective take on why you should read this collection.

If you'll allow me to tell you, from my unabashedly biased position as Charly's friend, why I believe you should read *Validate Me*, it is because Charly gives voice to the things we think but never manage to say. She gives expression to the intangible qualities of loneliness and alienation in this superficially connected world, and in doing so she makes us feel heard. More than that, she makes us feel understood. She probes darkness with the same tenderness as she tests the light, from the position of someone who has experienced severe and debilitating episodes of depression, but who has found the strength never to let this illness define her wholeness.

The book you have in your hands is precious. It will make you laugh. It will make you cry. It will make you nod your head in affirmation. And when you turn the final page, it will make you understand a little bit more of what it is to be human.

Introduction

Are you the friend that takes sweet secret gratification in others' failures? Do you like to indulge in delicious disastrous irony? How about oxymorons? Do you have a few moments to spare to flick through a book that warrants no need for more attention than a glance at your phone? Or perhaps – here's the clincher – are you a person that has a 4G connection and is currently alive on this here planet?

If you answered yes to any of the above, please take a seat whilst you sign away a few precious cells of your brain to the validation of my mental breakdown. A little scribble of thought with the tiny Argos pen you stole in your childhood is all I need. With that too take your own validation, you're a climate change warrior, that could've been single use. Can I get you anything? A dog meme? An old photo of Paul Danan off his tits? A Trump tweet to make you question what is left of this already heavy and futile opinion on life? Well, get up and get it yourself because I am currently circling around Praed Street, Paddington, London, dictating this into my phone having just strolled out of Accident and Emergency with little but an offer of self-sectioning and a plastic festival-like wristband with my name and date of birth on it as a keepsake. I am busy and now you are too, so Lady Gaga and Piers Morgan can wait, we have got a lot to try and decipher about how it got this far.

Nothing riles me more [this is a lie as you're about to read a book which is essentially a long list of things that rile me to the point of medication punctuated only by rhyme and the rare smatter of hope] than an introduction whereby the writer refers to the infancy of the book's process. It leaves me with a bored, bourgeois sour taste of someone else's self-importance, but as I've been hailed as an #instapoet I fear I owe it to some sanctimonious troll to exceed a slither of expectation. So let us suck the soured serotonin out of my life lemon.

I pre-empted this. I knew almost so certainly I was on the cusp of complete digital burnout that I pitched this collection thinking I was saving myself from it. Charly from the past, all omniscient, and evidently omnipotent, cackled her way through a Google doc, tripping over a cocktail of www.woes that she knew were exhausting but perhaps important and valid and witty, and hit send. Charly from the past but a few weeks later delighted at the idea of being able to use poetic licence for the first time in her sad, sad life. What fun! You need not sell the last fragment of your young and underdeveloped soul and past trauma! You can use FORESIGHT! And now Charly in the present is furiously walking to Marylebone station at 5am because her contactless card doesn't work so she can't get the tube and is desperately aware that everyone is staring at her in the night before's party dress, mascara on her chin and a hospital bracelet. She's also talking into her phone in third person, so I need not break this to tell you how far away from the grand dreams of poetic licence she is. This collection, albeit caricatured, is true. Some of it was written on grand spanking highs in expensive hotels in Los Angeles where I (ever the optimist in irony) searched for physical validation, a boyfriend, stardom and a good Instagram opportunity; some of it in bed wheezy on Venlafaxine, Propranolol and an algorithm that hates my content; some of it in Ubers and on trains; some of it to the soundtrack of the men in my local, little countryside pub; some of it leaving a hospital working out if I shouldn't have run away from it. But all of it was written on my phone and all of it is because of the curse of exactly that.

There. That's how we got here. This thing in my hand that stole all of my smarts so it could preface its own name with them.

Hello, my name is Charly Cox and I am code-dependent. So would you please, please just validate me.

My rhetoric is changing
My need for love confused
I've lost my inner monologue
And sold it all for views.

Click to Accept the Terms and Conditions

Shout a little louder

Come a little closer

Let me lead you to the void

The blank expanse

Let yourself fly in a seat

That is pants

Boom across a room

That cares for you little

Wipe off a slick

Of your new hungry spittle

That we'll sell you as gold

Come grab a feel

Of a hand you can't hold

Come be a person

That you never knew

Feel grand and feel gorgeous

Then feel worthless and through

Take a trip down the tubes

Get settled in

Welcome, you've signed up

It's all about to begin.

Objectify me

Validate Me Part 1

Thought as much
Famed as such
Faked the touch
Of what excites us
Who we are and will always be
Unites us
But we seldom invite that side enough
Swapped it out to sell new love
As though it's not inside us

Think too much
Fame is such
A thing we'll fake as something that excites us
Spin it until we're spinning plates we can't dine off
Starving
Is this what we'll die of?
Vapid monsters in a sea of breeding nonsense, jealousy
Portraits of unfulfilled and pretty
Best lives or misery
Rooted to mis-sold faith in a downloaded commodity
Do you like me?
Do you like me?
I don't know who I am any more
I don't know who you are
Fascinate me as I fabricate me

Castigate me as I congratulate me
Salivate as I let you navigate me
Masturbate at how inadequate I find me
I'm putting it all out to see
No idea of what I want or who I am sans vanity
No idea of how to please our grumbling society
No idea of where I can slip off silently
I am halves with who I'm wholly miscalculating
Please, would you just validate me?

#candid

You only take photos when you think something might die
You only post photos hoping that it'll survive.

#fitspo

Smelling of fags and biscuits
Embers the colour of the bits that I missed.

The Party

The door opens quickly just as my earring falls out and breaks. Steph catches it and puts it in her pocket, seamlessly, and stares confidently at the man leaning and swaying on the frame. 'We're here for the party. Right house?' She says this with a vague tone of annoyance because it's bastard-freezing outside. Neither of us have tights on and he's just stood there gawping, assessing, working out if he'll get off with one of us by the dregs of the evening. Music crawls in muted tendrils down the tall staircase behind him. No bass.

'Well, hello girls. Who are you then?' An over-exaggerated mockney accent dribbles down his polo; when had people started to think that being mindful of your privilege meant performing a class act?

'This isn't Mahiki, mate. Let us in, would you?' It wasn't, thank God. It was a flat in Denmark Hill, with a door off to the back of a newsagents. Our legs are bare, shaking, and my mind clamours for space as it beats itself into a pulp wondering how I could've crammed another cigarette in-between the Uber and this unnecessary faux formality. 'Robbie invited us,' I say, meek in Steph's confidence, staring. I feel shiny. My face feels filled with obvious pores. I feel an intense fraudulence, which I'm sure is about to be exposed. I do not look like my photos. I am catfishing myself, at best. ''Course he did,' he stares at my boobs and Steph's legs. It feels almost like a compliment that neither of us would ever admit felt like one, we've spent enough time slagging off how Robbie always must be seen with the next hot girl and how he always has a line of them waiting, and how horribly disgusting and misogynistic that holds. But to be assumed to be one of them? An ego boost. 'So can we come in or what? Bloody hell.' This is boring.

'Yeah. Yeah, come up.' He steadies himself on the bannister and the noise of the party engulfs us as he swings open the kitchen door. Everyone stops for a moment.

'LADS! FOUND THESE TWO LOOKING FOR ROBBIE ON THE DOORSTEP,' he shouts with smackable smugness. Some roll their eyes whilst others cheer, others pay no attention at all and the girls move in closer to the men they're sat in front of.

'Drink?' Steph glares.

'Bathroom first. I'll sort out my face. Pour us one in there. Then let's give this a go.'

I hadn't been to a house party in years, the coy butterfly-sizzle of excitement about the hours of pre-game are lost and forgotten. Nothing about being stood in somebody else's bathroom with a cheap bottle of vodka between our legs felt naughty, it felt a bit grim and regressive. The fists banging on the door outside were not of rowdy teenagers who'd overdone it, not of new-found couples burrowing away for the night for a private snog, but of four thirty-year-olds after the cold, flat porcelain of the toilet to rack up lines of cocaine, which they'd later learn was actually ketamine. We let them bang.

'Remind me why we're here again?' Steph screws back on the cap of the vodka, wrestling with the cheap teeth on the cap that won't quite align. Impatient.

I ignore her, transfixed in my own reflection. I do not look like my photos and although I have spent countless lost, and wasted, hours studying the planes of my face to an almost scientific degree on my phone, it feels like the first time I'd really seen myself in months. Vulgar. Vile. I do not look like my photos. Of all the places to be incarcerated as a fraud, tonight's setting couldn't have been more perfect. As we'd walked flat-palmed, pushing doors in the dark to find the toilet, I had spotted five men I'd at some point matched with on Hinge or Bumble that had later gone on to ignore my witty, well-thought and, through a series of screenshots to friends, well-vetted opening lines. I had arrived at a place of uncloaking.

The banging becomes more incessant and grows to a kick that shoots the brass lock up and off its holder, the four men fall in crying with laughter, pulling each other down to pull themselves up in a twisted rugby scrum. I may not have looked like my pictures but they certainly didn't look like men. Little boys, still.

In the kitchen, it is much of the same tired scene we had left in the past of our pre-youth, where we were too young to be doing any of this at all but still stabbing at the perceived rituals of fun that we'd learned from films. Scattered plastic shells of shots and stepped-on crisps nestle deeper into the thin cracks of the wooden floor. No one here was having fun. Everyone is desperately ferrying around in a painted distraction, feigning merriment, if only to not feel cheated of the future they thought they'd be living for an hour or so. Thinking they'd have kids by now. A house. A holiday or two a year. A career. But here we were, acting fifteen, feeling forty-five, grappling for an artsy shot by the plugged-in disco lamp, rehashing unread articles that made one of us sound cultured and the other aggressive.

Empty.

Your Boyfriend in LA Loves Me from Across the Ocean

When was 'psycho' so sexy
Yet still castigated?
Everyone here is married
But they're all fucking, faking
When was dumbing it down
Cashing in as enough?
Who sold you the fear
That you need to be seen as in love?

They grin doe-eyed and warm
In every photo you post
Happy Valentine's, Babe
I Love You The Most
It all screens so perfect
But I scream DENIAL
Am I bitter and twisted?
Just crave a number to dial?

Scroll

Where are you finding these partners?
Will you teach me your rules?
What do you serve them for starters?
Are you drugging these fools?

How are they harnessed
So tight to your hip?

Bzzzzzzzzzzzz

Oh
A DM!
'I miss you gorgeous'
. . . sorry love, it's him.

Mercury in Retrograde

We are ruled by
A fool's literature
Our settled Sunday readings
Map out an astrology-pulled apology
For the curves and quirks in our hapless week's psychology

Clutching a passionate grasp around instruction
That limits our habits to the moon's and sun's seduction
We are led by the hand, willing participants in our own abduction
Lured by the romance of another world's aura – chunked
construction

Running blind from our own control
Two thirsty dogs lapping from a cosmic bowl
Two sapient dogs lassoing a leash to their own soul
Dutifully bowing to boldly meditate
Around Leo's planetary heavyweights
Obediently howling at a weekly Mailchimp email to celebrate
A half-hashed understanding of Mercury retrograde

Cocking a leg to salute a sold faith
Doesn't the whole infinite eclectic point sort of dissipate
When we hand a stranger a title that lets them control our
own fate?

'I Know I Can't Talk but . . .'

Darling
You and I are important
And what I thought to be suffering
Was an inkling and a drain
But what the world around you is doing
Is seldom progressive
Just shouting SAME
SHAME
SHAME
Never looking back at the woman
Who was privileged enough to realise
Those sentiments were a gain.

#whatafeministlookslike

Dyed of its natural conditions
Died of its misconvictions.

Aesthetic

The glamour is better
When you're less put together
It's real it is felt
It's authentic
All that you are and all you exude
Weighs out its aesthetic.

Self Care

There is only a trace of anaesthetic
In the aesthetics
There is no truth, no freedom
No Holy Spirit's leading
In the clang of rose-gold copper self care
There is only growth in muddled despair
There is help in the hurting
In the muddied soul searching
In pulling it all out of mind for your eyes to see
It's mad – a cruel charade
For anyone to sell back your sanity
In bubble baths
Face masks
And breakfast in a bowl from Anthropologie.

The Walk-In Centre

Looking around, brush strokes of broad bored glances, everyone looks perfectly healthy. A little ruddy-cheeked from the December air and a faint suggestion of office-party regret, but no one looks like they are dying. Not that I know what the early stages of dying look like, but there is a disappointing lack of green gills, limbs hanging off, and intestines snaking the floor like stomped-on internal telephone wires. I suppose they think the same of me. Able-bodied, aggressively highlighted cheeks, bags of late Christmas shopping (the Urban Outfitters sale starts on the 20th so why bother buying all your crap prior?) and a fake limp so bad that I catch eyes with one man who gifts me a gentle ticklish cough, pulling it from his throat in solidarity, and we both do an awkward inward laugh. Ah, communion.

There is a lump on the back of my knee, which WebMD suggests is likely to be stage IV cancer or a golfing injury. I don't play golf. I am clearly dying. I wonder if everyone else here has convinced themselves that they are dying too? WebMD has become a form of idle procrastination for me, sometimes even when I am perfectly fine I'll click the parts of the digitised body and input symptoms just to see what they amount to. If they have any correlation. I am certain now that any time when I feel an organ fizz, I've got a spot on my right cheek or my ankles click, I can do some sort of WebMD-informed maths to convince myself I have a terminal illness. There is something about finding logical, even though it's not, impermanence to life that soothes my anxiety. There is something about finding pattern and reasoning in my body's shortcomings, and potential failings, that makes the notion of a suicidal thought seem quite quaint when I can convince myself my body is ready to give up before I give it permission to.

Not that long ago mental illness, albeit taboo and often dismissed even when as real and as profound as someone with suicidal ideation – there was a certain sympathetic coup for it. An arm rub. A waft of misunderstanding that means it is serious. Yes, it was saved for nutters and mad women, but it was also serious. There were institutes. Slurs. But now it just feels assumed. I don't feel any new communion with the movement of celebrities 'admitting' their anxiety and depression, I feel annoyed. I feel 'fuck'. There's already next-to-no resource, what happens now more people use it? It also feels a bit self-aggrandising. This idea of admitting.

The hero worship that would come off the back of it. I hate it. In a world so saturated for content, this feels like the new obvious like-worthy filler. Draw it out on an Obama-style YES WE CAN poster and it could be 2008 again. My illness isn't Kony. So fuck off. Depression and anxiety feels cancerous to me, but it no longer sounds like a killer. We've all got it. We're all being sold it in a breath of good deed and a lack of education. In fact, it's not different to how it once was. We still know nothing, the pharmaceutical companies are rubbing their hands, and we're all still mad and not being taken seriously. Only now everyone's being mis-sold their mental health, the thing we've all got and all must look after, as though it's an illness. As though we're all broken. As though any quirk or human emotion is a defect. So sometimes I like to convince myself there's something more physical, more appalling sounding, more known, so I can get a week off. Or a life off. So I can explain my struggles to an apparently new woke world in a way that gets some proper sympathy instead of a #MeToo. It sounds awful I know, but sat in this surgery, staring down faces who also don't look like death, I apply the 1-in-5 statistic and realise at least ten of us are here because of our brains. Ten. And I'm here saying it's cancer because my real killer doesn't feel real and I wonder who else is doing the same. I daren't say it to anyone ever because I sound worse than a climate change denier. I sound ungrateful. But in a realm of fake news and sold thought, that feels about as radical and free as I can think. How sad.

I shuffle about once my name's been called, ferrying heavy bags and a comedy limp to greet the doctor.

'I know! I know! I'm coming in with a leg problem and here I am with all these heavy bags like I can handle it!' I'm lying, apologetic, and unable to hear the echoing irony that will ring once she's read my medical records and knows how to properly understand them, if she can.

'Take a seat, love. I'll ask you a few questions and then I'll have a feel to see what's the matter.'

A feel to see what's the matter. Brilliant. Unzip me from the ears and watch like ticker tape as it falls, celebratory around my knee lump. Therein lies the problem!

She transforms from doctor to mouse, sheepishly suggesting that I have a womb.

'I have to ask this to all females, sorry – is there any possibility of you being pregnant?'

I love that she must disclose this as a run-of-the-mill question, as though once a woman walked in and complained to someone that they thought she was an easy whore who had unprotected sex, and was deduced as such from sitting in front of her GP.

'I bloody hope not.'

In-Between

Protruding
From both brain and skin
Seeping hungered odour
Someone please comment
'She's so thin!'
I want the worry now
I want anxious stares
Dreaming up
What once was there
I no longer want to be a half
One meal sounds plenty
I'll only ever make it
When my body meets my mind
And they feel the same: empty

I won't say it
It's not progressive
But it's streaming in aggressive
With every post
I am rewarded for being confessive
But my honesty now feels like boasts
They don't sound worrying
My body though not deemed extreme
Too small to warrant pressure

Too big to feel so mean
Wrecks itself unseen
In a sea of good-willed positives
Why do I now feel too in-between?

Snakes

You spit and you spit
Until there is no more
Ankles bound in venom
Piles of your innards bile
Across the floor
You never knew the fool that you'd become
The sort to be bitten by riposte
And for it to have sunk in and almost won.

Tubes

I fumble for my headphones
Snakes amidst the mess
My fingers untangle, furiously
As you shake your head

It swings, a nod come gesture
You jitter with your hands
You smile and look straight through my soul
I move rings to suggest I have a man

Music 'on', the signal's gone
I tap my feet to what I can't hear
The safety of knowing you won't say
'You alright, darlin'?'
Because there's white plastic in my ear.

Bad Feminist

I need to feel sexy
I need to be strong
I need to be assertive
In my right to be wrong
I'm confused, I've got lost
Am I the woman that I wanted?
Am I hashing out ideals
All excuses – fair of plaudit

Do I shout the loudest?
Were these things I had on a list
That my womanness was afraid to profess
Because I felt they couldn't coexist
Or
Have I passified myself
By defining my integrity
As believing that every thought I own
Is nothing more than internalised misogyny?

I've been angry
                  I've strangled fear
I've beaten at the ceiling
                       I've pulled quotes and statistics near
I've fought, I've yelled, I've felt

I've demanded
I've tried to help

But sometimes it all just feels imported
Is this my truest self
Or am I just a man-pleasing woman
Exhausted?

#spon

It used to be tits
Nestled in headlines
A break from the crude?
Flip to page 3, check out the nude
It used to be lips
Sucking on Flakes
Want a dose of arousal?
Skip to the ad breaks
It used to be legs
On bonnets of cars
She'd only be seen
On the right arm
It used to be trashy
Demeaning and brutal
It all seemed so brazen
So obvious, so futile
We gained it all back
I felt so empowered
Until I realised sex still sells
But this time to me:
Young girls –
Vitamins and whey powder
Clothes that don't fit
On the bodies they sit
Cinched in and smoothed

Hungry eye glares removed
Just sexy
And tiny
Sexy and tiny
Soft, lithe and shiny.

Validate Me Part 2

So dreamless now that is all that is left
What and who and why to be
When nothing but the truth is far-fetched
How to feel when it all seems in reach
A dangling carrot stick of a life
With only The Cloud(s) underneath

Where to begin and how to see
Why to feel and who to be
What promises to land
What honesty laid bare to keep
A dangling carrot stick of a life
With limited data to glean

So dreamless and chaotic
In the best way
Leading the oppressed day
Into one that is knowledge
Trying to feed off the same grown
That everyone else has new forged
When did the pandemic become organic?
Why am I in a panic?
Goodness was once transparent
Not an assumed apparent
If not given in abundance

Cancelled! Finished! Abhorrent!

So dreamless now that is all that is left
So schemeless, yet that was once my success
So diminished in that goodness to invest
Frittered it away to an account with no salvageable interest

Nothing means less than what I detest
Try to confess
What I have left
So please please just
Validate me
I'm confused, I'm bereft
It's all I have left
This exhaustion, frank and spent
It's all I have left
So please please just
Validate me.

Love me

Acceptance is the First Step

My neck creaks and crunches in unison with the seemingly unending pop and ping of the notifications blurting from my phone. There is a microwave pun in there somewhere, but the second bottle of wine between me and my girlfriend assures that we won't find it on the tips of our tongues. Just more wine. We 'deserve' it. Or I do, specifically. She comforts me – reminding me that despite my relationship woes, the confusion and conflict of having to announce having a 'not-boyfriend', a man whom in every conventional sense is my boyfriend (he's stuck around for breakfast after spending the night at mine for four months for Christ's sake, as though that is a real status and one that I am complicit with), I can still behave as though I am a carefree singleton. It pops, it pings, again, again, an Instagram vibrate, a Tinder nudge.

Creak, crunch, pop, ping.

'Trying to keep eye contact with you is like attempting to stare at the horizon on the fucking Titanic, babe.'

I blame it on the new pillow I've been using. It's a bloody expensive one; but I didn't have to pay for it. A hashtag footed the bill. I cling to the brand partnership in conversation like a 90s pop star thrusting their first newspaper pap photo at a mate to show they're making it. To prove their career is setting off. To show they've got some kind of vague but tangible place in pop culture. My worth as a person, a writer. A free pillow.

'Just because it's free, doesn't mean you have to sleep with it.'
We both laugh. Wine. Perhaps too much.

'I've told people it's like an angel's bosom caressing my shoulder blades, I can't back out now, I'm building myself on authenticity. I am suffering for my art AND my money.'

I raise my glass and then roll my eyes back in disdain. I hate myself. The pillow *is* like an angel's bosom, right? I've probably just strained a muscle from five years of carrying my laptop in my handbag and sleeping on friends' sofas. How many pillows will it take to make rent?

She contorts her body to bend back on her chair and forces a double chin with elbows next to her ears to get a candid photo of me looking *fine* and *happy* in the restaurant we can't afford. The waiters are rude, the food is small, the other diners are thin and boring but there's a Shrigley painting behind my head and the bathrooms have rose-gold taps and exposed tile floors that will survive a season or two more.

I slide the two empty bottles of wine out of eyeshot. Drinking is bad for you. Did you know that more than a quarter of millennials don't drink? Bad for your brand. I reach for a cigarette.

Creak, crunch, pop, ping.

The night before, propped up in bed with the pillow, face aglow with the muted night-mode light, I realised I was going mad. I text several friends to let them know – a new WhatsApp group of my favoured, most-trusted women – a message littered with enough siren emojis to suggest a family death. 'One of you needs to take me out tomorrow night. It's URGENT.'

I was going *mad* and it was not my usual flavour of neurological illness, not my usual predisposed millennial anxiety nor a *bona fide* disorder. This was a downloaded, delusional madness. For the love of fuck, the one thing I'd promised myself I wouldn't let happen was happening and filtering through my body with each exposing swipe.

I had gifted myself a personal agreement in the midst of the good times, pre-empting the inevitable end (it is seemingly always inevitable), that I wouldn't become another one of those 'crazed bitches', the ones my father and ex-boyfriends spoke of. The ones so steeped in paranoia, doubt and fear that their wiring would jump start at the flash of a screen. They'd scream and slap and stomp about. They'd post passive-aggressive Facebook statuses, issue out thirst-trap photos across all platforms. They'd make a scene.

As I lay in bed next to my 'not-boyfriend', his arms wrapped tight around me as I slid my forefinger over my phone, I felt my character change. I was becoming Her. I tried to breathe through my nose, clench my thumbs, meditate to cherish the moment of being held, reinforce the feeling that one day I'd look back on this and miss it. But truly I wanted nothing more than to suffocate him with the pillow and march out with my hands on my head shouting: 'I know about the other women! I know you don't love me! And I know you think I'm fat and you cringe when I speak! And-and-and-I know that you're still on that app.'

I didn't know any of these things, not really. Not a single one. But I had my dwindling self-esteem and fervent state of paranoia to form a stealthy hunch. He owned a phone, it was all perfectly possible and all incredibly likely. I was wrecked and there it was. Laid bare. I had become the woman, the irrational psychopath, the sort of girl that a guy gets black-out drunk in front of the football to forget about.

Worse still, I was internally describing myself as such, I'd become the perfect portrait of the awful misogynistic paintings that the seemingly endless stream of fuckboys had sold to me as unreasonable and unattractive, and I was selling myself off to the gallery, pricing myself up to the patriarchy, banging nails in the wall to be hung willingly.

'Go on! Marvel at my emotional craze! Am I on my period? No. But my fertility app says PMS is likely right now, so IMAGINE WHAT I'LL BE ABLE TO AUCTION NEXT WEEK.'

Not even my half-hearted, I'll-turn-up-to-a-Trump-march-for-a-well-intentioned-placard-pose feminism wanted to interject. I was actually Her. Jesus, how do you hate yourself these days without offending yourself?

Politically exhausted, personally bereft, physically poised to pounce at sending 80 generic 'Hey, cool profile. Fancy a drink?' slurs across the dating apps I'd deleted weeks prior. But I saved my data and text the girls instead.

Bursting from the seams, an almost masochistic euphoria – a failed lover, a failed feminist, a failed brand ambassador – no longer conforming to the internet's ideals, good or bad. It took a mere four and a half minutes until I was back on my phone scrolling an endless cycle, whimpering for validation. I am code-dependent and consumed, longing to just be liked, pushing off the arms of real validation into the grips of repetitive strain disorder.

Creak, crunch, pop, ping.

Score

I won't stand for being tested
I am not a pupil
I am a friend, a lover
And even if you are testing upon which one of those I am
Test yourself
Don't text me.

Downloveable

You're always a Sunday
Even one I dread
But waking up on Monday
I'm not dead
And that's you
You're the realisation
Left on read
You're the tangible hope of life
You're the frustration of feeling so alive

You're the love I need
That I thought you'd denied
Until I stopped, sat in present
To see it was mine to decide

You're the love I need
That I thought you'd denied
But something so large, so overflowing
Can't be hinged on a reply

You were all the love I needed
That I chose to deny
When I was scared it was mine.

'Can a Machine Understand the Human Heart?'

I've googled in the future
I scroll back throughout your past
I live within a moment
Where I thought that this might last
I've read up on our horoscopes
Checked what your sex moves mean
But my heart's still in your bed
My head's still in your sheets
Where I counted seconds of your breath
That you snored across my nose
I still feel your legs
Seeking warmth from mine as opposed
To the heat you warmed yourself with
The fired confidence I'd never known
I shrunk to be a body
Not your fault, maybe his
Now no search word, stars aligned
Can make sense of feeling this
Can a machine understand the human heart?
What difference does it make
When clearly we both can't?

Push
Notifications

Happy birthday
I don't mean it
I hope it's awful
An empty bar
Because all your friends were on holiday
Happy birthday
I don't mean it
I hope your parents got confused
And text your sister instead
Happy birthday
I don't mean it
I hope you're filled with dread
That I got a push notification
To remind me you weren't dead
And I wished you were.

141

I called your old landline on withheld
Just in case
Just to see if everything had changed
Four years later
I woke up your mother
The number was the same
And she drew a panicked breath
And sober-sleep-spoke HELLO?
You used to tell me I was insane
I lay the phone beside my head, turning up the volume
HELLO? . . . HELLO?
I hear her impatience, footsteps crashing to crescendo
She swings on a door
Tired eyes audibly dragging on the floor
IT MUST BE FOR YOU, THEY WON'T SPEAK TO ME
My body rattled
My ears pricked
Heart still settled
Until
'What . . . why for me?'
HELLO?
HELLO?
It was you
I never had any intention of speaking
There were no questions keeping

Me awake

I just wanted to see if everything had changed

And I can only assume it hasn't

Midnight and you are not in bed

Midnight and we've hung up before things were said

Remember when we thought we could be in love?

Midnight I still call as secret

I will take this midnight slice

In its oddity and keep it.

Worlds apart yet still connected

If only when I called your mobile

You'd accept it.

Modern Love

Was it written for us
Before we unmasked its disguises?
Was it planned and then pieced apart
So we would build machines to find it?
Was it always there
Unbothered by missed encounters
Sitting sweet and patient
Whilst we text into the early hours?
Was it always this much admin?
Devoid of purity
What was love
Before you swiped right for me?

Born of Hope

Much like a parents' time

The best we had was before we could speak

Much like a parents' time
The most magical was before we knew each other, had picked
out names
But we didn't know how it would sound when we spoke our
first words
Despite the expectation
Notification kicks
Feeding my life thinking it would seep down umbilical to
make you fatter with me
I'd sing to you down a text like it would make you smarter

Pieces of me and the father too, pieces of anticipation
But you were born not mine.

A surrogate to hope and a mother to loss
Snatched on your final term
Given to someone more experienced
Much like a parent's time
The burnings of joy in the conception
The yearning for more physical communication

The praying for unconditional validation

The swings of highs and nervous lows, the wait of months, all nine

The irony not one bit lost

Booty Call

My hand sits flaccid in my lap
Limp with guilt that it's betrayed me
Conscious of the grip it stole
Lifted, to attention, obeying
A command I didn't give it
A force all of its own
It rose with such excitement
Before it knew what it was saying

The repercussion is a buzz
It's dangerous
Exciting
Until it falls between my legs
To shine what it's inviting

It's all so fleeting, but I feel shamed
I'm drunk and I know better
The truth is nothing
Conscience weak
My limbs have their own vendetta

It's still aglow
Dropped on the floor
A fool

A slut
I'm dumb
I should've known from the beginning
It would've taken more for him to come.

Discover Page

I wander, wonder, walk for hours
Procrastinate
Forget the running water, cold shower
From sat to hunched to on my back
Feet in the air, nonplussed to sad
It stops me in my untraced tracks
Index poised, a gentle tap
There she is, a face I know
Burning me through a cold glow
A name I've written in my mind
Yours there too, indelibly signed
You're no longer mine
I've seen what you refuse to say
You're no longer mine.

#bestself

I don't want to be you anymore
Syncopated heartbeats
Throat tied up tight and dragged across the floor
I've been studying myself for days
Staring down
An entire ache
Life dulled to eye sores
I don't want to be you anymore
Whoever whatever why ever she is
I've been studying my ways
Sifting through their online archive
I haven't seen myself for days.

Overseas

It's mad where they'll bring you
It's mad where you'll go
Offshore with no confidence
Just entirely alone
5000 miles from home
I'm documenting it so you will see
A pointless performative charade
When for the first time in months
We're sharing the same city
It's mad what you do
Strung up in a toneless assumption:
That if you throw yourself out there
Really live with some gumption
That the words that you thought were
All laid out in blue shapes
Could read as a compass
Pulling towards a new space

It's mad when you get there
And it all ends so swiftly
Just a ten-minute phone call
Spluttered, selfish and sickly
That the power of what's in your hands
Is not the device nor that of a man's.

It's how you pick yourself up
And reassess this strange place
To know you still own your own map
And perhaps this is fate.

Elvis

He warned us of the fools who fell
But where is the wisdom to the persistent
To those who've ritualised their morning thoughts
To eighty new men
Their Singha beer tank tops
And David Attenborough dream dinner guests
Looking for nothing too serious
No one who takes themselves that way
Someone to listen to the time in Thailand
They got caught up in a cartel
Had their lives changed for the better, anyway
He warned us of the fools who fell
But where is the wisdom for the downloaded
Demanded, diligent, demeaned love dreamers who stumble
Nobody could croon it, no compassion possible
I wish Elvis had lived to see Bumble.

Obsessed

Last seen:
9:16 am.
Wake up,
Stop sleeping
And forgetting about me.

'Typing . . .'

Hovered,   hesitant
The thin line flashes
I exhaust the   pause
Until it's silent no more
And you are forced to expel everything you mean.

Glowing

When you wake your eyes are drawn to the screen
And I imagine all the people before us
Who didn't have these things
Who'd have lazed and lounged and gazed
Touched and smiled and yawned and snaked
I don't need your hand in the street
I don't need our parents to meet
I don't need *6 months* as a feat
I just want to know that all that's between us
Beneath the sheets
Is your eyes and mine
Our legs intertwined
Instead of waking up to you on your sodding phone.

Fake Muse

I matched with a model
Surely it can't be
What on earth would a model
Ever see in me?
He asked me out for dinner
Suggested we met at his
Turned out he was actually 56
5ft 4 with 3 kids.

#girlboss

Why does a prefix
Equal characters, equal weight
Become the thing that stirs and shakes
Boss would be enough
If we were just fucking paid the same.

The Break-Up

No sentiments sweet nor sour enough, no explanation worthy, no justification, no justice. As I woke to smugly catch my alarm before it had set off, a text had already set in. The months of wondering when we would both finally commit, take the grand leap of faith to monogamy, of which whilst I told myself I had already arrived at, knew truly, my digital actions spoke otherwise – **over.**

I had always thought myself a connoisseur of heartbreak, so very good at feeling melancholy and victimised, so very talented at believing I was born from a line of princesses trapped in towers with no saviour but alas, no more. I was strangled in fear, smothered by the truth. All that I had put off now emboldened in front of me with a back light. It wasn't what was said, the punctuation was not in the phrasing nor in the truths, it was how it had been delivered. A text.

The cowardice stung and raged through my body, ravaging away at each synapse that once heated to glow potential and future and fondness, now sizzling to rage. Occasionally cooling to anguish. I put my phone back under my pillow and sobbed, salty strings of wet and snot.

I had enjoyed living in a wistful denial, I had become so comfortable and freed in its endless confines of performance work and Cheshire grins and having someone to talk about casually in conversation. The significant lack of pressure from having a significantly silhouetted significant other, I relished in excusing all of the unhealthy and damaging lacking pieces because at least, in anecdote, they were still present pieces. Month upon month of carefully spinning my own web of comfort around the eight-legged beast of truth, not in malice or for love of deception, but so desperately caught up in feeling the validation of being seen to be in love. Of kidding myself my worth amounted to being of worth to someone else, and being of worth to others too. I knew, too, that no sympathy would come of this, and why should it? I had willingly and knowingly put myself here deep within an expanse that at some point had to start closing in.

These feelings, whilst felt but so perpetuated and manufactured, had to eventually learn their own language to scream back asking not to be abused any longer. A fool's game. I had birthed a Frankensteinian form of love and the bolts that kept its head together were unscrewing themselves. This was not a heartbreak that I knew how to deal with nor how to process, it was such deep shame and mortification. It, like the goodness I thought pervaded, took hold of my sanity.

Eventually, I got out of bed, I got myself here. Stood on the platform.

It terrifies me, resolutely, every time I see it. What if it just buffers me off? What if I'm not quick enough? What if I catch the driver's stare and change my mind and only get my ankle decapitated? What if I can't kill myself properly. A failure at killing myself. They'd love that.

'She couldn't even get that right.' Slap it on a list under tax returns and cooking rice, uploading at the optimum audience retention time and replying to anyone, ever. My inner rhetoric still so skewed to speak and perform to others even when it was pushing at itself. Nobody could read my mind here, nobody cared. It ranted in thirty different voices as to how my end would be perceived if it even happened.

I let it go on and on until it was hoarse, exhausted, until it felt different. All of the wild sparking mental chatter and doubt sparking until it was gone, everything just still. I stood in it. Breathe in for eight, hold for eight, breathe out. Nonplussed in the gust of hot Bakerloo Line air making hard acquaintance with the headlights in my mind's eye. I felt nothing at all. Just present. I forgot for all of six fleeting, flashing seconds, everything. In this moment I was just a really terribly sad person, an inconvenience to commuters, that was clutching at the tip of a final straw sitting in cyanide. Feeling present was only an inch easier than feeling like someone who cased together all of those thoughts.

I got out when I could bear signalless distraction no longer and walked to a corner shop at the end of a road I could only identify as a place I'd once seen bleary-eyed at an off hour of the morning leaving a man's house after predictable and sloppy drunk one-time sex. I smirked. I wondered if I got a map of London and scribbled all the streets I'd only ever been to once for regrettable encounters if it'd make a fun artefact for future older me to reference when I was missing my youth. I smirked again. Jesus, I was nearly smiling. Wriggling around in the gentle and genuine hilarity of making fun things for future me when I had zero intention of lasting the next four hours.

'Twenty b&h blues and that delicious looking bottle of tequila please.' Surely no one could be miserable when sipping from a tiny plastic novelty sombrero. Life science. Surely.

'How old are you?' the man behind the counter grumbled, hardly turning his head from the small portable TV he'd made little effort to conceal in an old crisp box. It was barking out broken sound bites of *Takeshi's Castle*. How the fuck had he managed to find a channel still showing it? Impressive. I decided I liked him.

'Twenty-three in four days.'

He swivelled round fully to assess the facts. A quick once over, up and down eyes that stopped efficiently at my cleavage.

'Lucky you.' he said, no smile.

I liked him no longer. 'Lucky?' Pah!

'I remember that age. Celebrating nothing but all the time.'

I'd passed without even fingering for my provisional licence. He gifted me my official title as an adult and then placed my other equally-as-important incidentals into a Colgate striped bag, nodded his head as the satisfying beep of the contactless payment authorising rung through to release me.

'Have a really lovely evening.' I didn't care about his evening much at all but it helped with the charade. I had got very good at being a convincing shadow of a happy, put-together person through being aggressively polite to my core. He'd already turned back to his screen, safe in the knowledge that I wasn't the sort of person to be skulking underground considering my meagre life options. I was a 'lucky' young girl with a plastic bag of tricks and fun with a whole Friday night ahead of me. What could there possibly be to worry about?

'Where are you?' Thirty texts blimped in. Almost all of them question marks. 'Helloooo??'

'Ok I'm getting worried now.'

'Why is your phone off?'

'Wait, have you blocked me?'

Hazed, I slumped against the wall of the shop, I was just staring, not really reading. He continued to type.

'OH THANK GOD, they've gone through. Sorry. I thought you'd died or something lol.'

There had been many, many points in our non-relationship where 'lol' had frustrated me to a point of lobbing my phone from one side of my bedroom to the other, screaming muffled into my white knuckled fists. Lol, simply put, was the death of us. Lol, more poignantly put, was the disconnect and crack in conversation which he'd chisel every time I wanted to talk about anything that warranted more emotional lineage than the meme he was hell bent on picking apart. Three letters, taunting, the most inane piece of punctuation. How do you reply to lol? How do you come back from it? You don't. Lol is where lots of love comes to die and, in turn, almost me.

Another text, pushing me to the ends. I wanted to call him, fall to my knees and scream, 'You BRUTE. You've done this. How could you possibly end all of this over a text? Is that all I was? Nine months! A text! Done! Over!' but soon realised, with a few words rearranged, a few time stamps altered, that was exactly what I should've been shouting at myself.

#woke

I woke up this morning
Misinterpreted my privilege
I'll tell you I'm mourning.

Suffocate me

Selfish Care

My will-he-won't-he relationship had been officially he-won't for a few weeks and in-between convincing myself I was dying of terminal illness, loathing the bones of my body, and incurring incredibly impressive debt to Deliveroo and Klarna, it was the sight of his name that churned my insides in the most cruel and undignified way. I had been avoiding department stores (and now, even my beloved Duty Free) in terror: one stray squirt of his aftershave could kick the backs of my knees in and have a pristine woman from behind the beauty counter calling security, gagging me with her silk neckerchief as I smash each bottle off the shelf like a T-Rex who'd finally afforded his arm extension op.

'A sample, Madam?'

'A sample of nauseatingly happy times? Get stuffed, mate.' I couldn't risk it.

But the other places lingered under my nose still, the other places not only unavoidable but greeting me with every waking second as though they were doing me a kindness. 'Suggested' lists, unopened voicemails, photos begging to have the faces recognised, filling my body with the most putrid acid, concocting another cocktail in my stomach. So far down in the pit of my intestines it was almost comically a shooting pain in my rectum. Anxiety, leading the way to remind me of what he really was.

The melodrama of my every thought and sense had pursued me to Heathrow, one 11-hour flight away from freedom of heart.

It had chased me down with such aggression that asylum was all I had left. The notion of feeling so uncomfortable and rigid had become a certain kind of comfortable – one that I was frightened to keep seeking comfort in. Perhaps, I thought, if I unleashed myself to the swell of spontaneity, just like all other good bourgeois heroes of mine whose stories I'd dogeared and underlined and idolised, perhaps if I forced myself to truly just ~live~, I would be able to recapture a sanity so long ago felt. I can hardly help myself as I walk through the connecting flight tunnel and before I turn my phone off I hit send on a tweet that simply says 'Goodbye, strange world.'

'Good.' I think. 'Ambiguous.' I think. 'My friends might worry, strangers might offer sympathy.' I think. 'This buys me some time, to see if anyone really, truly, actually cares.'

Flight mode on.

It's selfish and it reeks, but no more than the man who sits himself behind me and reclines his seat barefoot and rests a toe on the arm of my chair, I reason, half convinced. I suppose when given the opportunity to do as we please and block out the immediate consequence, we are all the same.

I unpack my kit meticulously. Oils and self-heating eye masks, miniscule sample pots that have been labelled with numbers to ensure they are slapped on in the right order. One book on leadership (I have never worked in an office), a copy of *Letters of Ted Hughes* (it is almost the weight of my check-in luggage and I, for the most part, hate Ted Hughes), a notebook (laden with past haunting memories best left unchecked up on and with few pages left to make any real new notes) and my laptop (of which I have idly forgotten to charge enough to watch all three series of *The Durrells*). I wish so desperately I had a to-share bag of chocolate buttons, a Sally Rooney and some cheap make-up wipes. The young woman next to me eyes it all up, salivating from Drunk Elephant to Chantecaille, head cocked at Parker pen and Google Pixelbook, opening her mouth at Ted –

'That's quite an impressive spread you've got going on – you're, like, professional at long haul.'

I smile, accomplished. She asks to take a photo of it, accomplishment.

Ferrying back and forth from the toilet at a great rate of knots, there are so many damned steps to kidding myself that this is a well-earned indulgence, I have wasted three hours and missed the food trolley twice by the time I've ripped the perforated line of lavender sleep aid, but it has caught the eyes of several other female passengers, all stopping when they do eventually catch me in the line for the loo (again), to ask what hyaluronic acid I use. I don't, but I mutter something about The Ordinary over Glossier with cool nonchalance and trudge back to my seat much more disgruntled dervish at the thought of having to get up to wipe whatever heavy muck I've just slicked under my eyes and left all over the sink during turbulence than serene wafting angel of essential oil and inner clarity and calm. I am kidding myself of total connoisseur-ship; it feels so good, all velvety and lux, the idea that other women value my opinion without knowing an ounce of what sits behind my silk sleep mask. It has all risen to a perfect and intricate soufflé of me perhaps being the lost daughter of an Eve Babitz-type on her way to storm Beverly Hills. In an instant I can imagine the wealthy old men I plan to prop myself up on a barside with, the old-fashioned way, to humour and engage with and, as my great-grandmother once joked, leave a banana peel out for once we had inevitably got married much to society's shame and mockery. I could even see my own reflection in my black patent Louboutins, wiping a single solitary tear that miraculously leaves no mascara, clutching a silk pocket square that he owned well before I was born. What a farce. I take half a Propranolol when I think about how much it all cost, forcing me into a haze of whisky, comatose. It turns out all I needed to relax was, in fact, my medication.

I think a lot about whether or not anyone will have seen my tweet yet. What time is it at home and did anyone remember I was leaving? Those who don't know me, do they think I've died? I hope they don't, I truly hope they don't, but there is a sprinkling of sociopath fizzing deep down inside of me – someone that once started off moderately concerned with content curation – that is rocketing against the walls of my soul waiting to full-on Berocca effervesce into that kind of arsehole. Shit, maybe I already was. Shit, why on earth was this even a thought that I could begin to simplify, justify, in my head? How had I made up the face and the mind of someone who I was so far from with the organs and failings of someone I'd always been? When had I let the meshed veil enmesh into me? Whose funeral was I excited to wipe tears at?

I am Too Many Characters for This

When I wanted anything at all
But no one felt familiar
Or safe
Strangers felt the place

My teeth hurt from biting
A dull pulse

Close eyes
Drip

Drip

No one is awake to alert
I would not wake anyone to this state

Frightened

Absolutely fucking terrified

Close eyes

Drip

Bite

Are you awake?

No response

My last message can't be a tweet

My last words can't be public

But in the end

They would be anyway

As a warning

Close eyes

Drip.

4feiting Grandad

1

The ghosts that you see
Are me
Always at your foot
Crumpling the bed covers
Telling you what's for tea
As soon as
We can both swallow again

New-found cuts
So long hidden
Prick and sting
Smothered in silken anti-bac
Tiny slits that scream
I would endure a thousand more
To be sure that you'll come back

2

Gulping down diluted bitter lemon
We trace your gravy lips with paper
Your good hand squeezes, your bad hand holds
Us holding back on things you couldn't make
For what we'd give to take this all away
You think in new voices and speak the language you could save
Your good hand tickles, your bad hand holds

Out for connection in the days
The only thread you seem to pull
Is that when we're together things can pause
To sit and know
To sit and show
Memory-scapes of feelings will always light and love the same

3

Last Christmas I sat face deep in a text
Fearful of what our next interaction would be
And you laughed
And noticed
And I'm so angry I was so cowardly
And pushed away from asking you all the questions about
everything
And nestled into screen

And now
Every time I see the picture of us as my screensaver
I can't hear you laugh

I want to scream

4

The magic
So pure and undiluted
Of your laugh

The half
Of your smile
The prickle of the wry upturning
Of a presence unpresented for a while

The melted chocolate and Zovirax
Twisted on my finger
As I prod at lips and teeth
To feel a shape that had always been there
Just unprovoked

Four hours have passed
Time full with purpose and belonging
I haven't once looked at my phone.

Comparison

How did she get so beautiful
So struck with all the sharpest planes?
I'm stuck down in a lasting pain
What I would give
I wouldn't eat
To have that face, even her feet
Can't stand the sight of toes
But I'd pull mine off just for her nose
None of this is love
Not infatuation
Just sad self-degradation
I'd take it all and never give it back
Wear it like the only skin I've ever had
How did she get so beautiful?
How did I get this mad?

Convenience

It's a blessing!
What a miracle to be bestowed
Thai food and taxis
All straight from my phone!
How did I live before
Endless freedom and curry?
Oh right, of course
I used to have money.

Silent

What's winning about worry?
I just want silence to stand in
Wild and weary but working
Act with great abandon
I lay it to bed
Tucked it in cosy
Switched it to silent
Wondered IF ONLY
I could do this every day
To stop purging on thought
To sign a cross in the noughts
I act with great abandon

'Stop calling, I'm doing okay.'

Captions

Cigarettes don't taste the same
For minutes I don't know my name
My legs feel weak until I'm drunk
So this is it
I'm here I'm done

I try to turn it to something new
As though pain is a commodity
Lacking in inspiration
Struggling
This is the truth.

Priorities

I take comfort in the kisses
Not the real ones
No.
The digital missives
The Xs
The exes
An equal amount would be enough
Would I be so fucked up?
If I wanted to be text
As much as I needed to be loved.

Busy

In the darkest solitude
I'm still here, still me
Still available
To anyone who wants a piece
In the quiet, wrapped away
From first thing in the morning
Throughout the whole damn day
Even when I want some space
Or feel guilty taking it up
Even when I'm busy and stressed
Even when I'm making it up
To seem important
An innocent pressurised style of fraudulence
It's all one big fat lie
Really
I've forgotten how it feels to be alone
Or any independent feeling
I miss being lonely
Disconnected from being so connected
Never having a moment
To feel affected, dejected,
I've redefined rejected
From lack of being wanted

But before I know it

Phone calls, texts and WhatsApps
Tweets and likes and hearts to hand
Noise
It doesn't stop
I am held to be a subservient speaking piece
To something I can't turn off.

Switching Off

It burns. Half acid reflux, half Chinese wrist twist in the pit of my stomach. Momentarily, it pops and pings and it leaves my fists to clench tight around the plastic casing until I hurtle it across the room.

Please don't smash.

Please don't be important.

My fear of texts, emails, calls, notifications has now become physical. It's difficult to explain without likening the incoming vibration to a giant mythic monster that wants to devour me. I am reduced to this now, my internal monologue, my internal rhetoric, so obvious, so clichéd, so ready to be condensed into 160 characters. I feel trivialised by my own voice. 'Giant mythic monster that wants to devour me', what part of my brain did I just engage to think that sounded smart or profound? A box left cerebrally Sellotaped shut from the age of six? Give me strength.

Oh.

Off I go on a tangent.

What was making me miserable again?

Shit. It's ringing again. Even if I know it's a friend asking for coffee, my brain re-translates that information and swells it into panic. Hot nasty panic.

Unknown number?

Hell. No.

WhatsApp party invite?

I'm busy.

Text from a colleague?

I don't exist anymore.

At what point can I kid myself that, through being so drastically difficult to get hold of, I just don't exist? At what point does that become true? Whilst it is painful and boring for me, I am relentlessly scared of what others must make of it.

Rudeness.

Ignorance.

Callous, uncalled-for ghosting.

It's sad because it's not personal. I just find it so hard.

So hard.

Sometimes I imagine a life where I just didn't have a phone. Perhaps then I'd stop having to usher pitiful excuses months later about why I never called back. It's so far removed from care, from social interaction, that I can't get my head in or around it. I scroll my contacts when I make it into London to see who I can call for lunch.

No one.

I have avoided 80% of these numbers for months, why on earth would they want to eat the lunch I starved them of in February?

Shit, did I even cancel?

I am someone who constantly strives to avoid loneliness – I like the noise and clatter of loud chatter around a dinner table, I like being near people, I like exchanging stories and I like being a part of jokes and I like my friends. I like them a lot. So why has my phone made me so phobic? I just can't face it.

Occasionally I'll see a set of months where I'm relatively

unfazed, engaged in midnight texting and meme shares, but currently I'm not there. It is quick to escalate. One missed call becomes one unread text which then becomes another and another and another and another day of dread and fear that I've not replied.

Now I have to be silent on social media. I can't seem to be engaging in other parts of the digital world.

Then a week goes by and I've not posted a picture of my breakfast or reshared a pointed political article. Then sixty emails pour in.

Open one. Muster a reply, perhaps text one of 19 unread texts, promise drinks next Tuesday.

Facebook messenger pings.

Commit to dinner on Wednesday.

Monday comes and I am scared and exhausted again.

Cancel all plans.

Turn phone back off.

Repeat.

What's this inane bollocksing idiocy?

What's the under layer?

Anyone?

Does anyone know?

Maybe I should just keep it switched off.

Broken Abacus

I move my rings
From right to left
Like playing with an abacus
One finger with a perfect tan
The other pale in new absence
Absence
Abstinence
Passionless
By accident
Had not given it much analysis
But suddenly I'm stuck in a psyche paralysis
When the guy who's plonked down next to me at the bar
Surveys me
'Oh babe, you look fabulous
What are you drinking?'
And it's not that I am thankless
Nor was he particularly tactless
I fancied him, I really did
Absolutely no denying his handsomeness
Had this been 2017, this is where the night would've turned
quite scandalous
But I move my rings
From right to left
Like playing with an abacus
'Sorry darling, I'm engaged

But I appreciate the compliment.'
His eyes swing off from optimist and dominant
Now bitter, soured, unimpressed
He moves his seat and splutters 'boring'
I don't know why I did it but
I think maybe it's less morbid
To suggest I've already found love instead of
'I just don't have time for a mortgage.'
'I'd love a baby but I don't think I can afford it.'
'What if we do this for three months more
And you still won't call me your girlfriend?'
'Have a drink with you and fall in love and leave unscathed?'
'You're a man not a godsend.'
When did it all become life admin?
So confusing, complex, tricky
What happened to enchantment?
Oxytocin banging like confetti cannons
Having a traditional life trajectory
Imagine
I wonder if I had gone to school
Then university
Found my sweetheart
Then a flat
Got married, had a baby
Worked until I was 65
And died a few years later
If that was all a possibility

If that was attainable and expected of me
I'd leave my rings
Not need to count on them
But as one hand clasps my phone
And my fake engagement rock glistens
I realise I'd been so consumed by frustration
When fate called, I picked up but didn't listen
Romance used to start in bars
But I'd grown so used to the comfort of a screen
'WAIT, COME BACK. I'M SINGLE.'
I flap about and scream
But he's gone
The room fills with his
Absence
My abstinence
Passionless
By accident
I think I've got a broken abacus
Because none of this adds up
And none of this should matter.

Overshare

Personal and political
Controversial and hospitable
Frightened and empowered
Sleeping safer, but for hours
Pushing it out, locking it in
Fumbling for the end of the anecdote
Before it's had time to set in
Renting out space for others to sit
When all I want is a new one
Because this home is still sick.

Validate me

The Dinner Party

Regram the gifted
Who told it much better?
Who rehashed the clickbait much neater?
Who braved brevity
And got down on one knee
To marry an idea so desperate
Without meeting its parents?
Who cares for the source
When you can skim its matter of course
And still impress all of your friends?
They'd never dare question
Such a good-looking suggestion
For fear of not knowing enough
And having done the same.

Celebrity

I want the moon
I want the sky
I follow the stars
I want their shine

I want it all
All that's above me
I want nothing more
Than to be it and for them to love me

I want what I can't reach
I want all that I can see
I want the things that I can't touch
I want it all, I want so much!

I want! I want! I must! I must!

How foolish, silly, dumb and fucked
To salivate
To celebrate
Social divinity
When there's a piece already in me
What ignored-already fortune
What blinded, wasted luck.

Cary's Castle

You catwalk the bar
And head for the screen
Take off your sunglasses
A sigh a relief
Just mumbles of others
A curtain between
Sat entirely alone
Unmasked with huge swollen eyes
Feeling uncomfortably alive
Feeling finally seen
By no one but you
A sigh a relief
Finally seen
It's grim and it's snotty
It reeks of sweat and of sleep
It curdles within you
A rotten green pang
And then from out of the barrier
A stranger puts out his hand
You shrug off reluctant
He's killing your moment
But, actually, he's there
To properly show you it

'London!' his voice swells
'You must be an actress?'
Not quite, you reply, though this is definitely acting
'But your beauty, that accent, what's your success?'
I guess today I finally got out of bed
That's all there is
Everything else is a mess
'Kid,' he says, 'look,'
This guy is pulled straight from a film
'You've got yourself here
I saw you come over to hide, head bowed as you walked, I
know that stride, you needed to talk,
And I'll give it to you straight
You don't need to smile for the room
But put one on your face
Because what you feel inside
Is the best art that you'll make
It's all yours to keep
But it's getting you down because you've been giving it out
Instead of giving it chance to ruminate
I'm so glad I wasn't grown up in the digital age
Because I've learned that it's all much too easy to fade
When you're forced to dine out on gesture
Giving meals for those who weren't meant to take.'

Worth

It's not in the ether
Left to wriggle and writhe
It's not lost in your legs
Pouring out when they're lithe
It's not in your emails
It's not in your likes
It's out in your life
It's on the ground waiting
When you need to survive

Stories

They wore Shrimps
Ate a few
Passed around crystal glasses
Chinked, cheered and cherished
Until they fell on their arses
What a sight to behold

It was warm orange autumn
No greater deed than to
Fall back and relax
Cans of Stella, bags of crisps
BMXs and Vans and pillowed-up Eastpaks
What a sight to behold

She'd turned seven
There was cake
Balloons and party bags
They're making secret memories
One's they'd never think to brag
I wasn't invited
What a sight to behold
Though this one I couldn't see
Just left to imagine what I'd never have been told.

WHY WON'T YOU LIKE MY SELFIES??????

What I like the most
Is I know he never lies
His kindest vocabulary
Is locked in shrugs and sighs
Sweet loving eyes
That bind to mine
In honey
I sink down within it all
And let it all run off me
For as much as I could bathe
In all his unspoken compliments
Sometimes all I really want
Is for him to scream at me with confidence
To hit me that I'm stupid
To bash me that I'm smart
To strangle me until it's me who's mute
I'd take that as a start.

Monzo

Things of value used to last a lifetime
But now they're things that we regret
Feelings, cash, commodities
Mis-spent
Notified in a text.

All Reads are Good

For the love of Christ, Keats and Rupi
For the love of the lonely
For love of the only
Words that make us safe
Pick up this book
Pick up another
Just find comfort for comfort's sake

Slate it, slant it, sling it back
Cast it stupid, naive, unpretty
But one man's 'pile of precocious shit'
Is still allowed to be a young girl's favourite ditty.

Toby

I miss you so terribly
The pain of which I need not study
To understand
All my human data enmeshed
Sprawling axes and climbing charts
Coloured bars and kisses crossed
You learn me constantly
Consistently
Always present like this feeling
I miss you so terribly
So terribly it's almost lovely
So terribly I feel deserving
So terrible so lovely to know
That whilst your love is seldom simple
Your voice on a call
Always feels like home.

Trolls

Carnivorous and hungry
They're always out on the prowl
Don't care that you're happy just want to know how
So they can pull it from your clutches
Steal a piece for their own
Fighting bare skin and knuckles
Euphoric?
Step away from your phone.

The Instructions They Forgot to Give

Behind every fear is a wish
Behind every wish is a dream
Behind every panic
Every stop, start and flat line
Every reshuffle and standby
Is purpose
And longing
Behind every hour of hard work and solitude
Is the making of hours of future and evolving

Behind the people you detest
Putting your moral alignment to test
Behind digital deliberation
Behind dating frustration
Behind overwhelmed feeling
Behind every half try at success

Is purpose

Behind the days you feel worthless

Is purpose
It's clichéd and disgusting
It's sickly sweet
It's improbable and unlikely

That it'll ever present itself as neat
No unambition is exciting
Nor is it worth achieving
Nor is living out your dreams
Only when you're sleeping
What nonsense is living
Only a reality that's disbelieving
Your desires
Waking day to day
Putting out your heart's wildfires
Denying its purpose
Making time for the exhausted surplus
Of becoming the imposter
Growing up your insecurities
And leaving your best qualities unfostered

Behind being angry at others who are better
Behind being comfortable with shrugging off 'whatever'
Behind losing yourself to a constant anxiety
Is a purpose that's screaming for you to wake up
And see that behind every fear is a wish
And behind every wish is a dream
And behind all the things that you feel are obstacles
Is simply you putting an excuse in-between.

Instagram Boyfriend

You would sit
Marsupial
In the pocket of my Kooples
Jacket
Ready to pounce
Unironic
Tripod and macro gadgets
At the sight of stucco houses
To shoot me cardboard cut-out
Beatles walk
And make me feel
Liked and skinny/
Nonplussed look to the left/
#pretty.

Bath

Wrapped up in bed sheets
Mummy denied
Toes tipping and dipping to song
My eyes staring straight through the ceiling
To rest in the sky
He hits keys practiced but not languid
I try not to cry
At all that I've become since I was last here
My tongue flat bitten under teeth that are still furred with beer
And pride

Escape should feel dream-like
Ethereal
Weightless
Not scalding and visible
Not constant and pointless
Not at arm's reach when you should be sleeping
It should shudder out from your bones
It should press a pause in your thinking
Let you just be breathing
Just being
Some peace

That night
I sat down at his kitchen
For a moment I'd had time for a thought

'I'm being'
Not forced
Everything falls from my face
He smirks and calls it wisdom
But it feels more like a place
That I've been desperate to hold place in
Worked hard for money to have wasted
Trying to get there
Hours upon days, tapping, erasing
Flapping around in a haze
And calling it fashion
Calling it purpose
Calling it poetry
Calling it worse
Calling it escape
Calling it peace
When all it's been is piss paltry days
Of being stuck in modern ways

Not stupid, just learned
A manufactured calculated form
Of anxiety that is a dullness
Sizzling to fall and flatline as the norm
Beating myself up for not finding a way past it
So caught up in frustration that it's the only feeling that's lasting
Picking at pieces of the past begging them to be forecasting
But what has been and what isn't yours

Won't show you new
You can't simply expect peace in lieu
Of taking space to be it

Sometimes it takes waving surrender
Sitting down with kind eyes and with food
Sitting down with free hands
And to allow people to hold all of your weight
So there's a chance to make space inside of you
To allow people to hold all of your weight
Hold all of your being
So you can take it back again
And polish the peace that was always within you.

~Inspiring Quote on Backdrop of Ocean I'll Never Swim in~

I know we say
No pain no gain
But what I'm growing is a loss
Could it be a proverb unfinished
Or one with a last line that we forgot?

I know we say
No pain no gain
But is that what we really mean?
How about
No pain sounds nice
And gain is just for greed.

#instapoets

What's the point of having a good turn of phrase
When with it you've really got nothing to say.

The Conception

All pink and flesh and naked
All screams and kicks and brazen
All hope and wide eyes, anticipating
Grabbing hands for mother's milk and smiling faces
All life and all love and all bundled up
Precious and gentle and soft to touch
All new, all you knew, was all them and no you
No thoughts only feelings, all life, all love.

And so they grow you with hope and with wisdom
They pick you up when you fall
And when you're wounded, they kiss them
They force feed you greens
And obsess on your teeth
Mild on minding your manners
And wild on watching you breathe
All that was once them is now you underneath
All body and bones, all genes
Prematurely bequeathed

But you grow and it falters
And you find an opinion
You rage and you range from
Your own person to minion
It happens and happens

It has done for years
But this time is different
New pressures, new fears
New notions, ideas
New things pressed in palms
That are born not of tradition
New measures for tears
New motions, pioneers and careers
New directions to choose
An invite to take pride to prize in a new exhibition
With everything you've not even owned yet to lose

You're pacified with sugar-free and a screen
You're shielded from truth but have access to obscene
You're cuddled and loved
Until it's time for TV
Join the table for adults
But quick! Here's your iPad!
Before you start to scream

You've got a phone with no numbers
But know all the buttons
Know your own rights
Before you know comeuppance
Not yet, not quite
It's about to hit you in waves
Micro-aggressions

Radio slaves
Ultra pressure
Visible early graves

Kiss chase is long gone
The adoration assumed
Why keep the parameter playground
When it can be publicly consumed?
Bios littered with Xs, dates, hearts all on file
Profess your innocence adult
Forget that you're still a child.

#notredamn

'I went there on my gap yaaah –
#blessed, My tears still stream.
Here's an essay on its beauty
Five photos vignetted on me.'
Silenced only to the notion
That we care less to protect the future
Than we do to rebuild history.

Emails from Elizabeth

My phone had been half-touched for days. Hands that used to jitter and shake, pocket grab and stroke, now sat upon, occasionally pulling at eyes, mostly reaching for a glass of wine; until now.

Of all my pathetic and medical addictions, the obvious glaring things that come with pictures of sick babies and bleeding gums printed on packets, this one that I swore was beneficial and not a benefactor to the others, has risen up to reveal all of its truths. I am drinking more and smoking more, my body is now coffee and debt, I blame it all on the devil and idle hands that are punishing my lack of swipe and simpering. I blame its toxicity for the others' latent lure – that I am carefully forgetting all came long before it. All my other crutches felt, through my phone, like lovely little brushstrokes on a caricature of me, this ludicrously dressed mad woman always offering out a lighter and smudging spilt wine with the other hand, phone safely nestled in bra ready to whip out to digitise it in all of its glory, a portrait of posterity.

But without it, albeit a few days and albeit notably lost because of a pulsating anxiety behind each eyelid and heavy in throat and throb of limbs, that portrait no longer hung. Its gilded frame is simply empty wall. Those things alone were dirty and sad and desperate. They needed, they were alive, on the anecdote and laughter, the tapped-in postcodes and lofty, last minute WhatsApp plans. The pirate red lipstick-stained bad habits could only be dragged out of bed in this state by friendship. By communication. Perhaps, much like the other things I hated to love, it was me that was the perpetrator, I was the problem. My need to constantly wash out silence instead of really listening to the whirring inner monologue of crapped-on cogs. Distraction. That's all any of this boiled down was. A magician blaming its faulty tricks when he himself had not mastered the magic at all. I was killing the doves before they had chance to fly.

The next evening, as I stopped to sit and write this in the grandeur of a bar I had screenshotted so many interior shots of it no longer felt exciting to actually sit in, I deleted the tweet.

I braved my email. Braved! What a hero! Who was this modern-day saviour, so stoic and nouveau?! Surely not I. But it was. A subject line glared through me and my eyes welled up in elation. It was Elizabeth.

Elizabeth who I'd met twice but, knew within a fraction of the first instance and consolidated on the second, knew me beyond the facade. She met me as me and liked me as this half-hashed idea of an adult that I was trying to grow into and to when I ran away from myself in body and mind. Here she was without a lifeboat, but an email to drag me ashore. A little rubber dingy-shaped offering filled with love and hope and reality (reality!), speeding towards me in the horizon. I'd mentally waved the white flag, brain just sparks of panic flare, I bloody well needed this days ago, I had received this days ago, but it was me who had denied it.

The doves started to flutter, all white and crisp and mesmeric, the dancing line that flashed and taunted after each new word that had legs to be absolution pulled at its chain, a new word, a new line, a new admission, a new honest recount of the dismal place my brain had reached, pulling pulling pulling, wings flapping and flapping and flapping until it felt such a cruelty to let them struggle any longer whilst they had such pure and powering intentions of freedom. So I let them. Before I shut off their wings back into my faulty box and lay furious that the words I needed had been waiting for me all along, the connection, the communion, I let them flap and fly to reply.

The back and forth, mammoth paragraphs of encouragement and update, lit me with all the things I had been hoping to find by running away and turning everything off. It dawned continuously, a buffering morning, that nearly everything that had happened, great and devastating, but with concentration on the great, had been possible because of the online world that I had grown up in and become so dependent on. Before my dependence, of which I was both to blame and a product of society, it had initially looked to me to be pearlescent gates that I owned the key to unlock whenever I needed to skip through and find something that I couldn't find anywhere else.

The nights at fourteen that turned into early mornings, making friends on forums discussing boys, and on many occasions saving strangers from the things that they couldn't bear to tell their parents or closest friends. The endless meme share and laughs and frankly incriminating WhatsApp messages that solved even the most intricate maladies. Photos found and reblogged that pushed me to believe perhaps one day I could take and one day did. Recipe blogs that proved to me cooking delicious meals was attainable, within my reach, good for my mind and my body. WikiHow that taught me, somewhat shockingly much later than I care to admit, you can in fact wee with a tampon in. WebMD that had convinced me of ailments that would later make them money, but also validate my symptoms that I couldn't articulate in real life and give me a second chance. The dating apps that joined me with heartbreak but also with now best friends of whom I know certainly I would not still be alive to write this without. The confidence that I had previously used it with, not a crutch, but as a tool, had shaped me to be the person sat alone in a bar five thousand miles from home, heartbroken and lost, sad and defeated, but with someone to pull me out and hope to keep me going. The former were things I was in control of and had lost hold of. The latter, a gift from the very thing that I had spent so long castigating that I could pick and choose the direction of but had held too firmly.

I flail from my bar stool and catwalk to the loo. I announce it to the suited waiter, 'Just popping to the loo!' and he laughs as I knew he would because they think it's charming and British and I know it's crass and uninteresting. It feels a half a step forward to acceptance. I am crass and uninteresting and somewhere deep down I love that, I hope.

The bathroom itself is incredibly opulent, the walls are coated in a flaked gold leaf and the mirrors have the sort of back light I would assume most 14 year olds now are able to fix to their front cameras. My eyes look tired, a bit drunk. But they upturn slightly as they survey each orange patch on my collar where my foundation has run from sweating and crying, sweating with anxiety of realisation, crying at the relief of just that. I tug at it and then laugh and then cry again and then sweat some more at the prospect of this very image existing on someone's CCTV footage. I half want to ask if I could get a copy, my brain whirring at what sort of Tracey Emin performance piece I could make this and then I stop.

I had placed my bag in the sink and had taken no caution as to think that a toilet as fancy as this one would likely have sensored taps. My bag filled with water and I just sort of watched it. I didn't flinch. After much, much too long, I picked out my belongings from the basin and smiled. Had I totally lost the plot? Or had I finally, like Andy in *The Devil Wears Prada*, thrown her phone into a Parisian fountain and realised I absolutely had the power to stop my life being so unbelievably miserable for the sake of appeasing a beast that the world worshipped but did me no good?

The transformation had been done. The portrait complete. I was an Anne Hathaway meme.

I, albeit totally penniless, albeit totally heartbroken, albeit five thousand miles from my actual home, had refound place and had taken back accountability. A product of all the things I thought so wrong had made me into enough of a person to turn them into riot acts of rights that I could now scream.

I don't want to have to say

'AM I RIGHT, LADIES?'

But

It is better to have loved and lost, than to never have loved at all. It is also better to resent something so passionately and then see it was just a mirror, than to have never owned a phone at all.

Am I right, ladies?

. . . answers please on the back of a postcard.

#bodypositive

I like my body when I've eaten very little
I like my body when it's shared with other people
I like my body, not often, just sometimes
I like my body when my body isn't mine.

Acknowledgements

My heartfelt thanks to everyone who has unfortunately encountered me online and in real life. This book felt impossible to write so many times and these thanks go to those who spurred on the most difficult parts of my adult and professional life thus far.

To Kate Fox, your patience is unrivalled. I cannot thank you enough for the undeserved kindness and perseverance you've shown me. Anything, ANYTHING that is good and makes sense in this book is because of you. Thank you for indulging me, thank you for making me feel like I could finish this when I really really felt I couldn't, and for never judging me. For your compassion and understanding. Thank you for validating me.

To Lucy, from the depths of Epsom to the depths of my heart. To the lengths of my love to the proof of your talent in the awards that you've won. I hope we get to travel the country eating Percy Pigs and listening to pop music for as long as I can afford to keep you.

To Celia, I love you. Thank you. You gave me the confidence to continue on this journey, you gifted me the damn lot of this.

To Mum, your support and love and cuddles. Your strength and wit and belief and passion. The woman you are. More. Always. To my family, always.

To my favourites at The Royal Standard, one day I'll write a sitcom about you beautiful idiots, but until then here's proof I wasn't just staring at my phone but I was ACTUALLY writing a book instead of buying you a pint. Bizarrely, and I hate to say it, you've kept me sane.

To DJ and KB, heaven knows where we'd be without the night we didn't know what to wear. The Vaginas till the end. Harry Winks forever. Us, until WhatsApp gets taken over by something else and we all reconvene.

To Tirion. To you. Always, forever, for the rest of our lives. I could never put into words why this book is a product of you and why I love you so much, those endless MSN nights. So let me buy you a Disaronno and cry at you instead. Thank you.

To Kasey and Brittany, your friendship and your support makes me so grateful, so happy, so filled with everything I so often lack. But when I see your names appear on my feed, I am okay again.

To every girl I ever met on A2AA chat, staying up and talking about George Sampson made me so much less alone, so much more accepting of being 14, it also made me believe that one day I'd write some words that weren't just lyrics to a George song he'd never see. I am forever indebted. You kept me alive without knowing.

To Sam W, I am sorry for all I've put you through. But I love you. I love you so much. And I'm sorry that I do. Here's another book with some poems about you.

To Toby, to Clare and to Simon, thank you for everything. For making Bath feel like home. For feasts and for warmth. And for giving me the courage and inspiration and Alex and Jane to finish this book. I truly cannot thank you enough.

To Adrian, always. You are the beginnings and ends of my world. Digitised and real. I wouldn't trade your sing song down the phone for anything. Not a thing. You're my other half in this world, I'm so sorry that I might be yours.

To Finn, charge up those ear pods. I'm calling you in 10 minutes. Thank you, always.

To Billy. It started with a poem, it continued with us crying our eyes out in West Hollywood. They say you shouldn't work with children or animals, I'm glad I took the risk and worked with both.

To Brian, without your emotional intelligence and fortitude, without our beloved sports bar, you and I both know more than anyone this book would not have been possible.

To Louise aka Luis Dedknapp. For opening up. For the nights out that reminded me I shouldn't be in. For helping me feel sexy again. For your friendship and our kinship. For everything. For us.

To Elizabeth, I fear to write any more for you without you imposing a restraining order. #Gramie forever and know always whatever flowers are on your doorstep, or whatever love you feel anonymously, it's from me. Thank you for much before you knew me, you are why I write.

To Agent Abigail, thank you for not giving up on me. Thank you for your patience. THANK YOU.

To Jackson Davies, for showing me strength, for showing me power, for showing me LA. I love you, nugget.

And finally, to every stranger turned friend who bought me a drink, showered me in kindness and offered advice on Sunset Blvd. The whole damn stretch of it. Thank you. Thank you, thank you, thank you.